Swear Words

Adult Coloring Book

ISBN-13: 978-1530607372

ISBN-10: 153060737X

All enquiries, contact

Potty Mouth Publishing

pottymouthpublishing@gmail.com

Hello and welcome to our first swear word adult coloring book. This book intends to help you relax and unwind after a hard day at work…or at home. Just let yourself go, and enjoy some very juicy, sweary words coloring designs.

We have tried to collect a mixture of less common but nonetheless very naughty curse words to shock you, surprise you and make you smile…this is an "adult coloring book" in the truest sense of the word.

Enjoy your naughty side, get your favorite coloring tools and start relaxing with swear words adult coloring books by Potty Mouth Publishing.

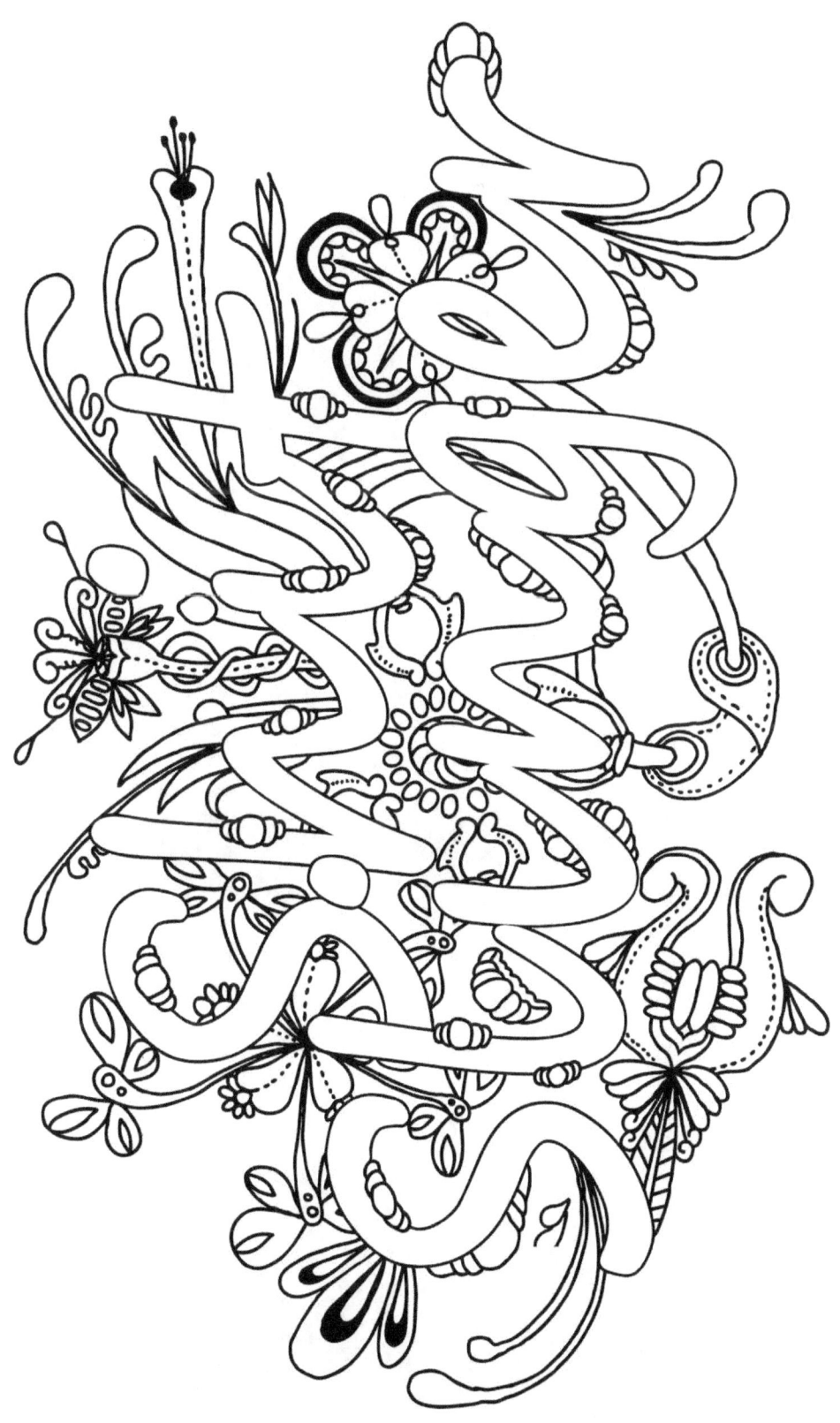

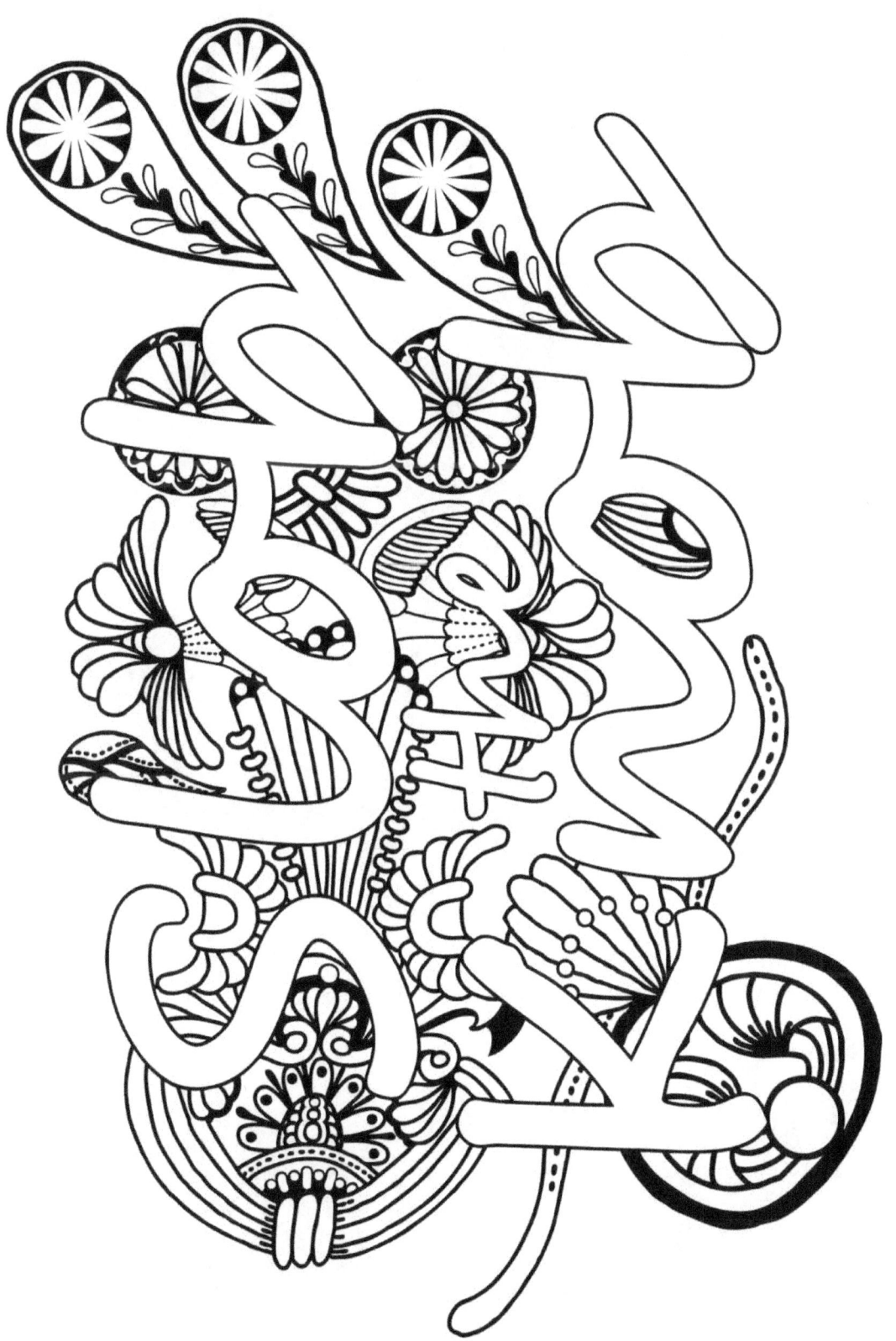

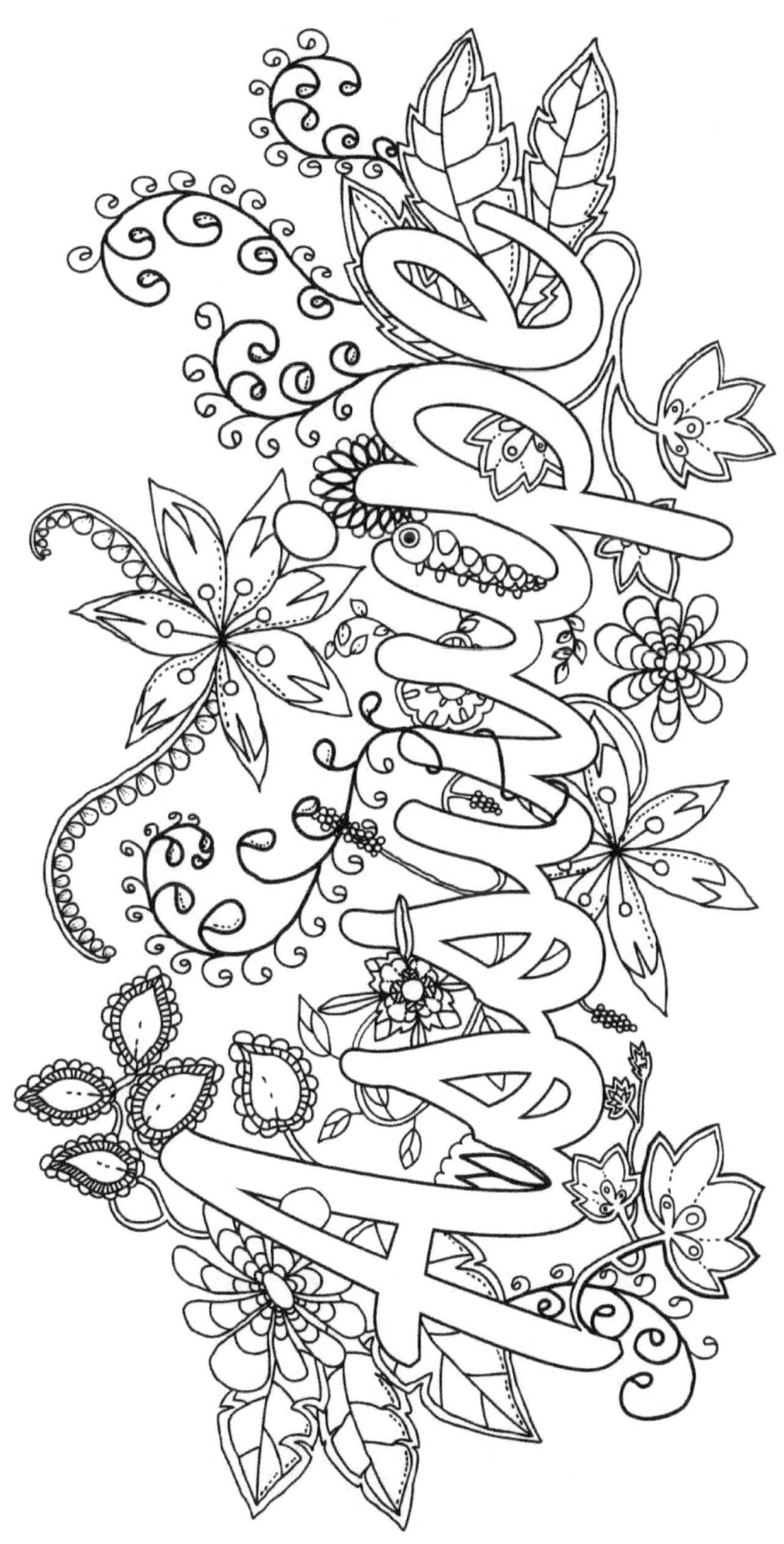

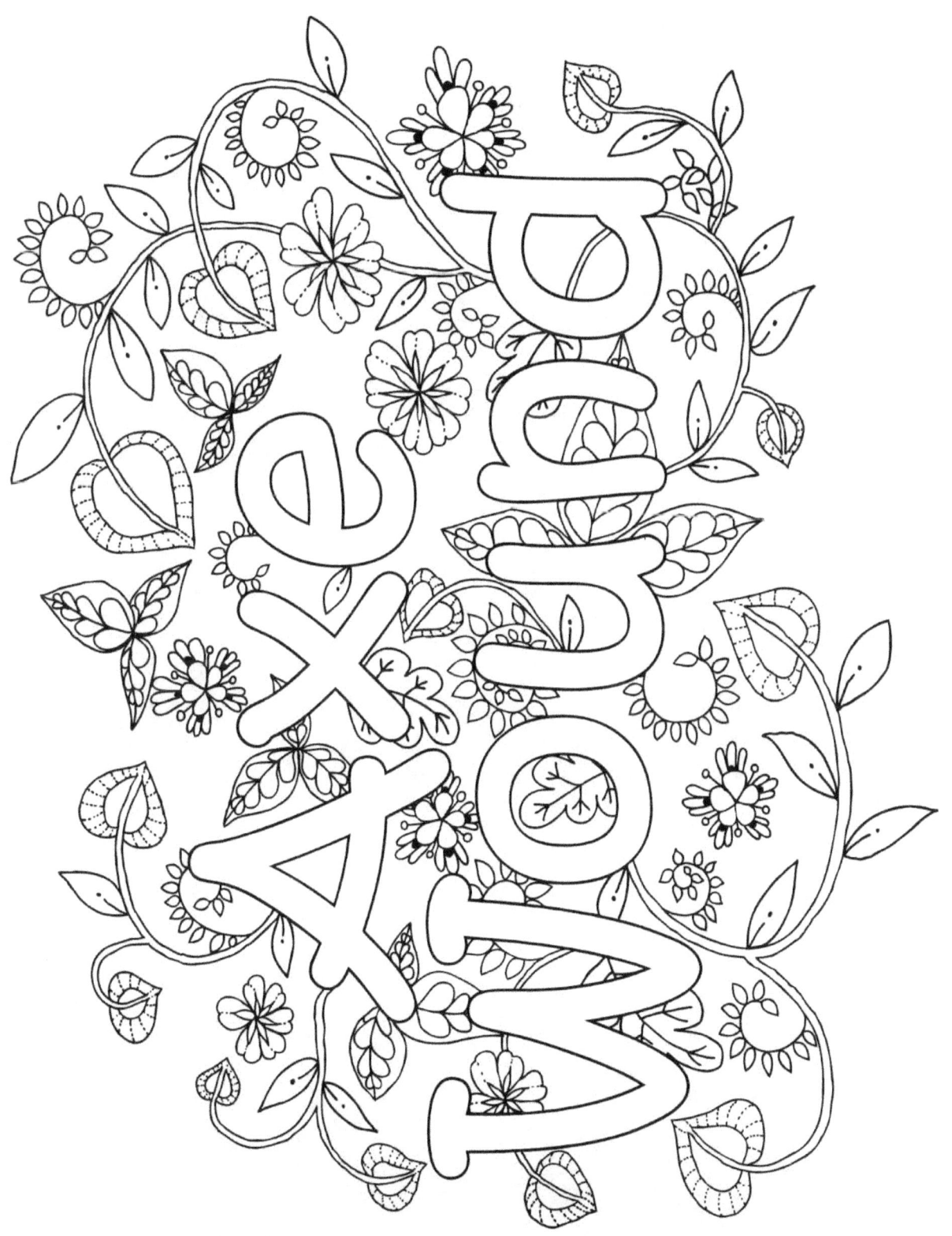

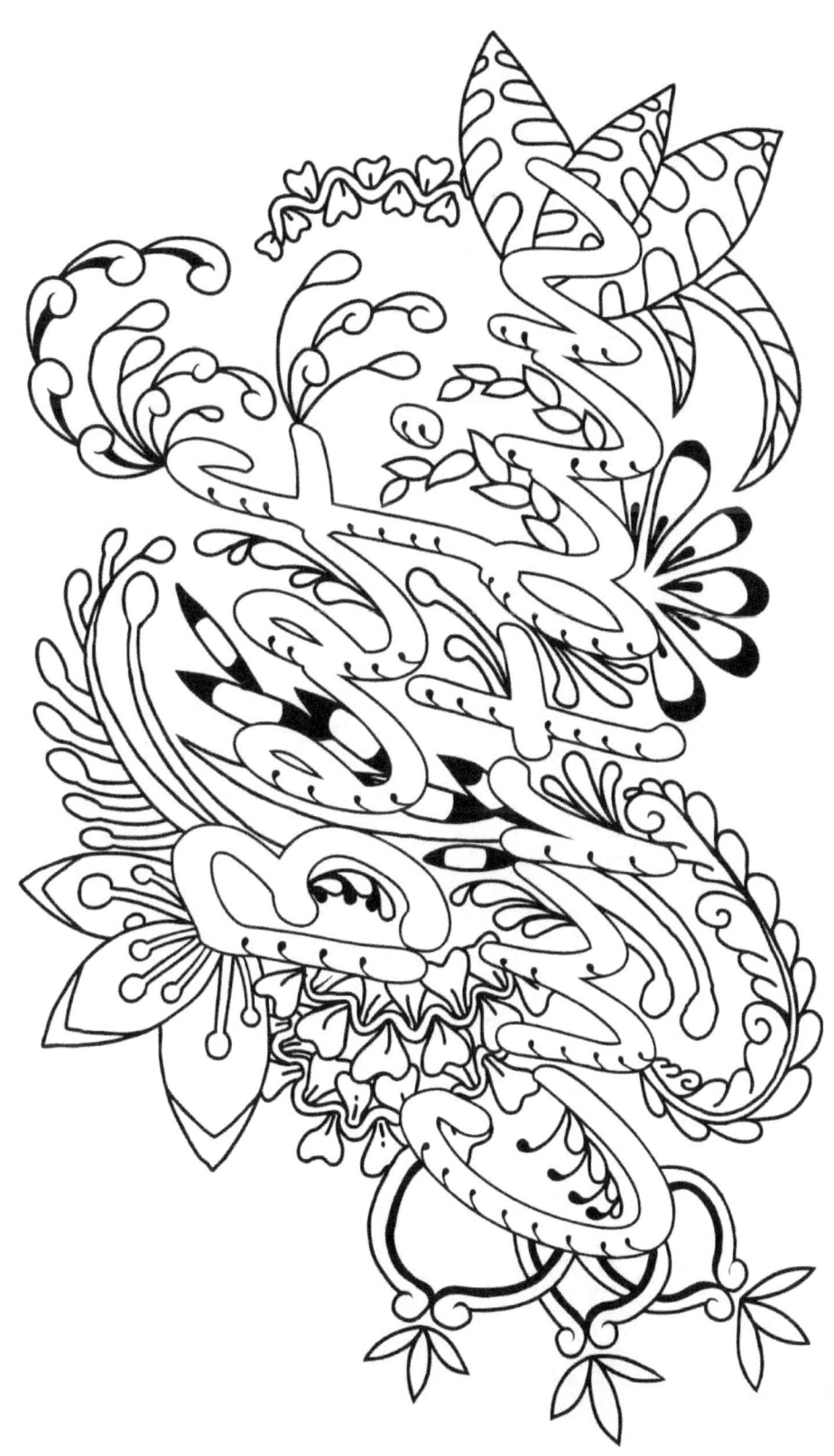

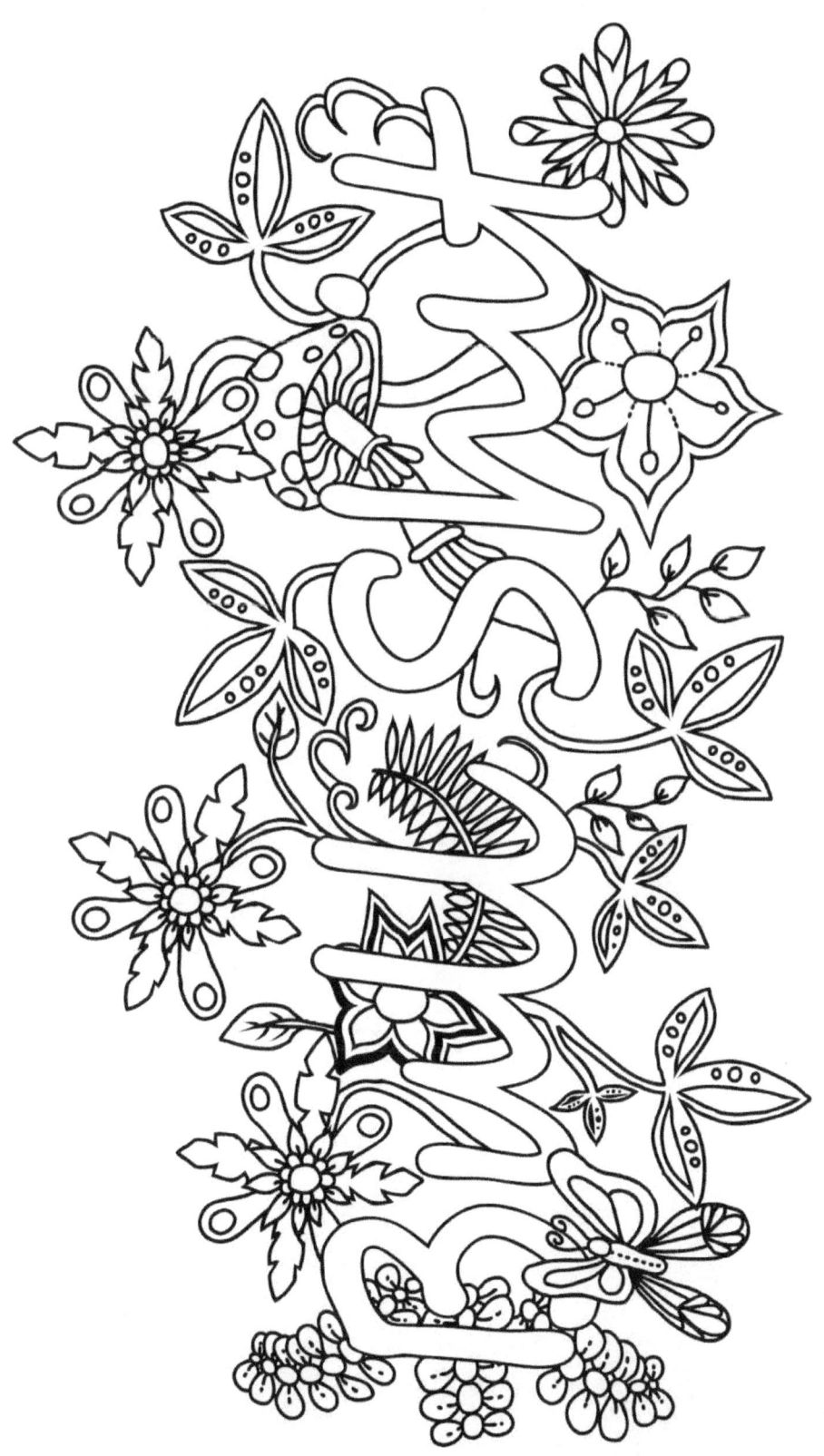

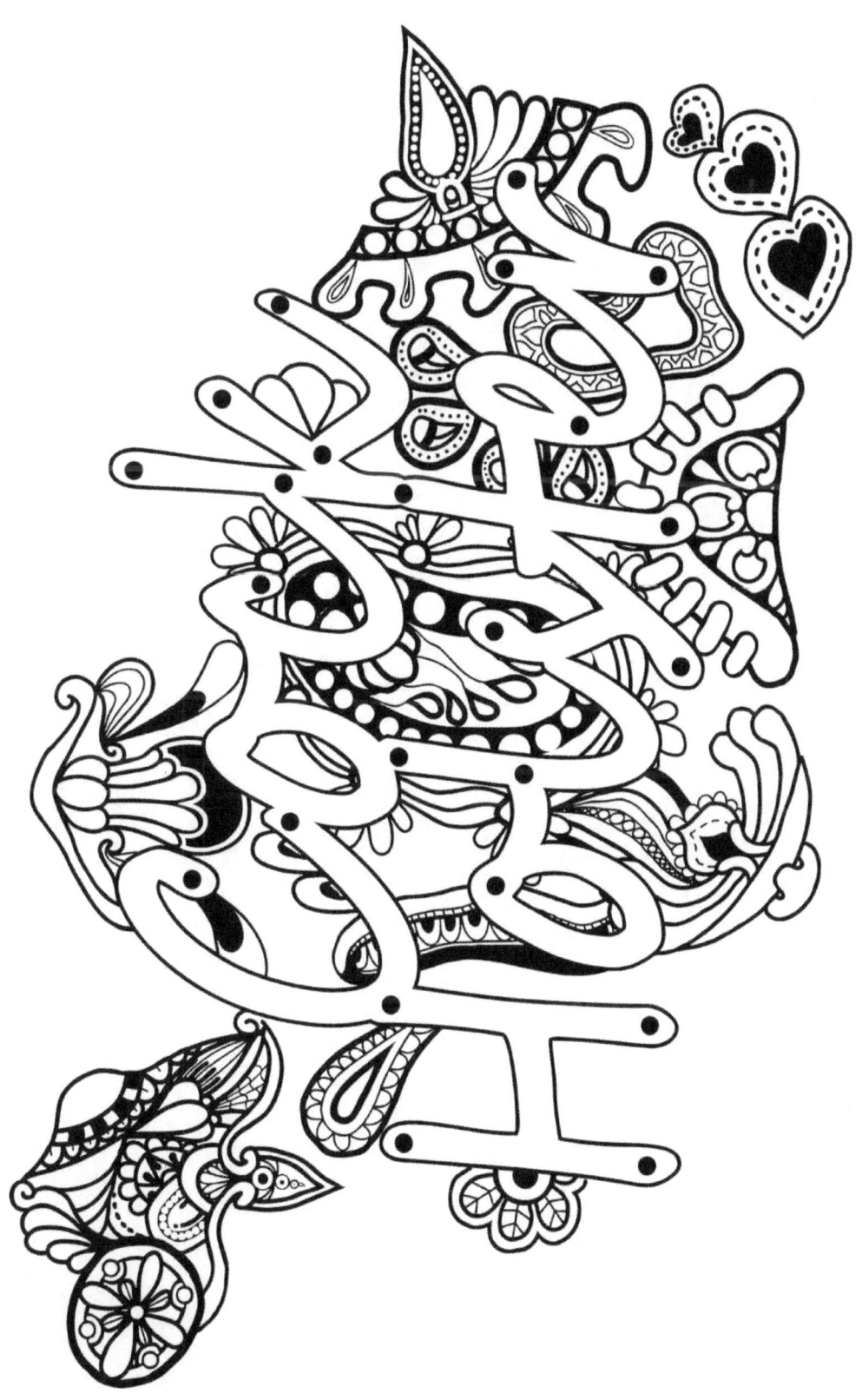

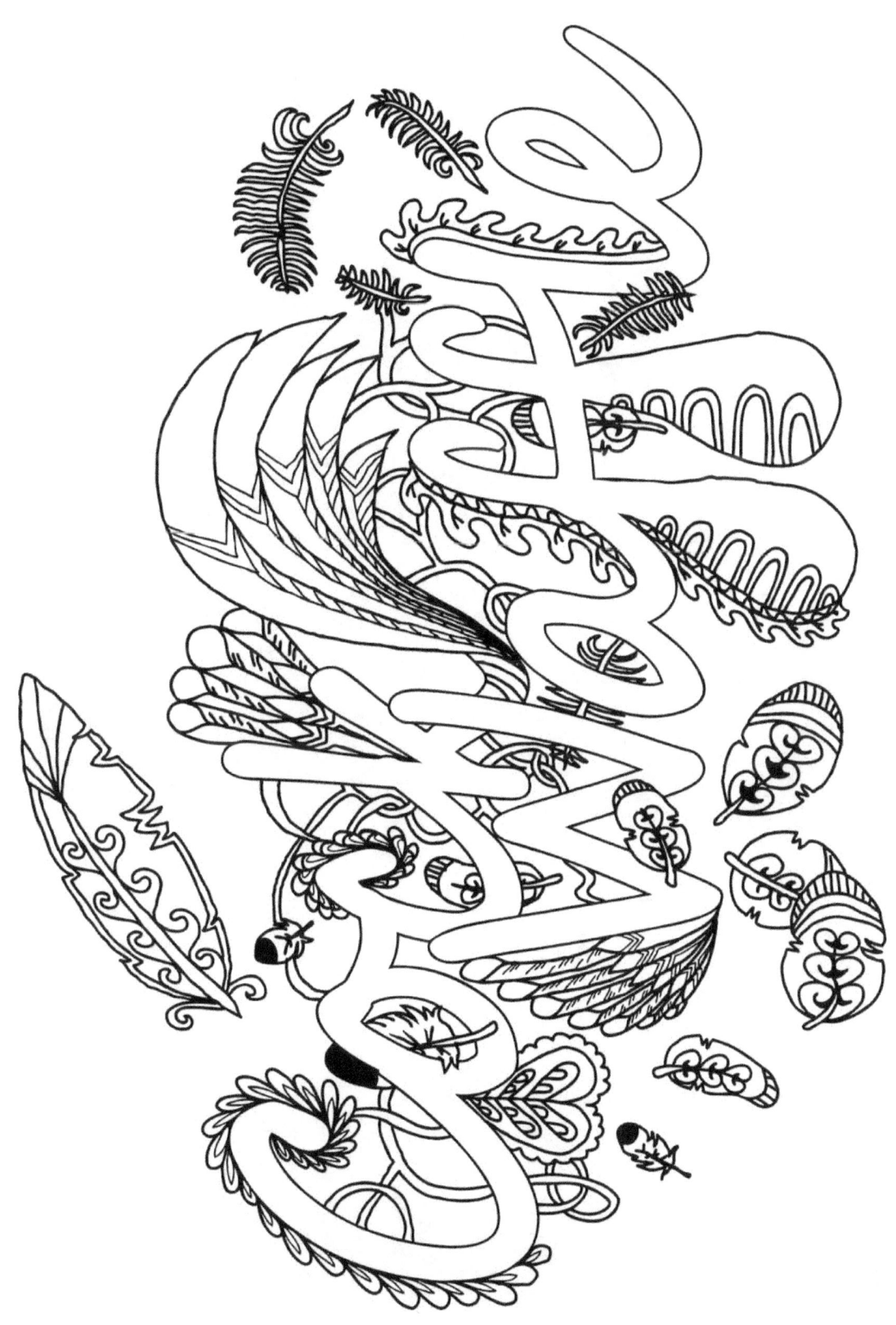

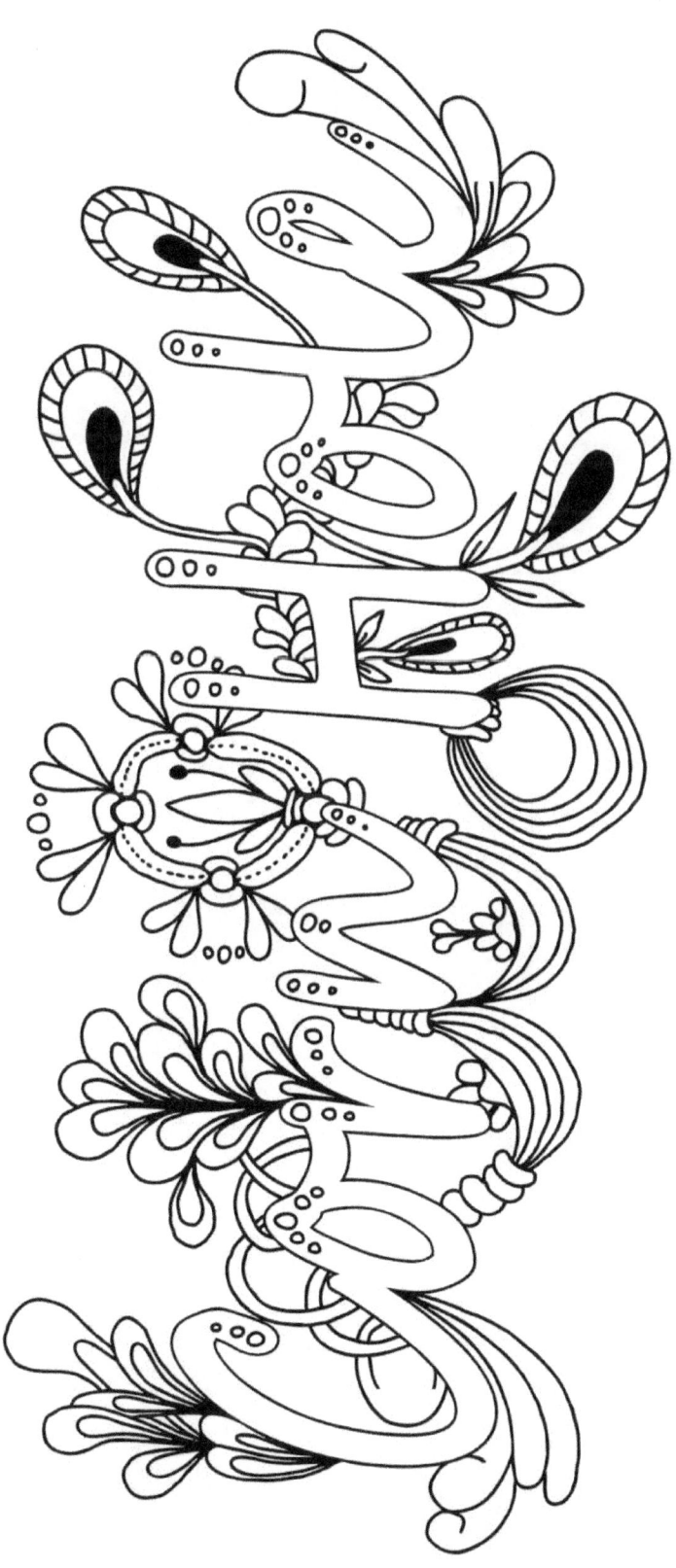

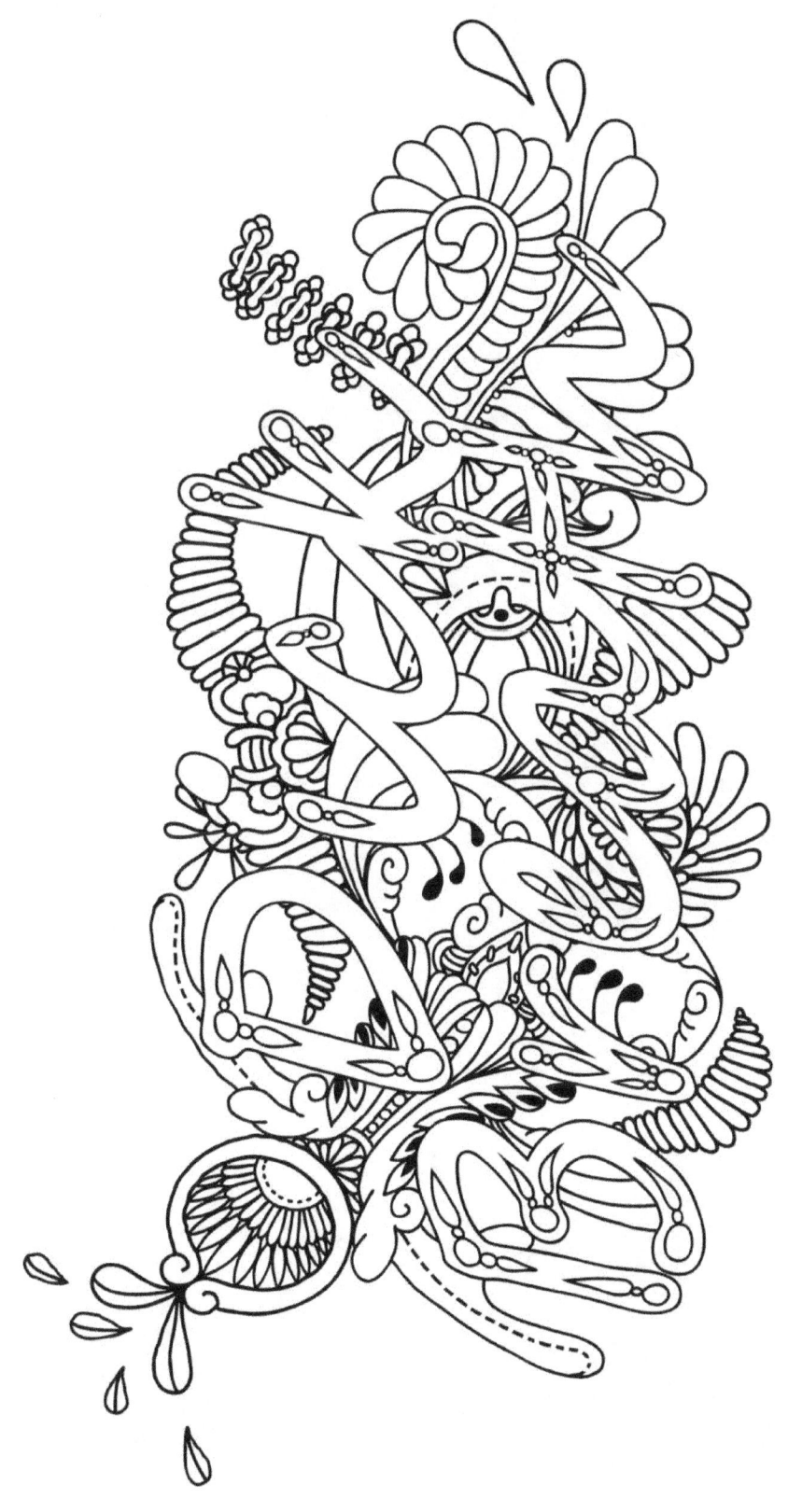

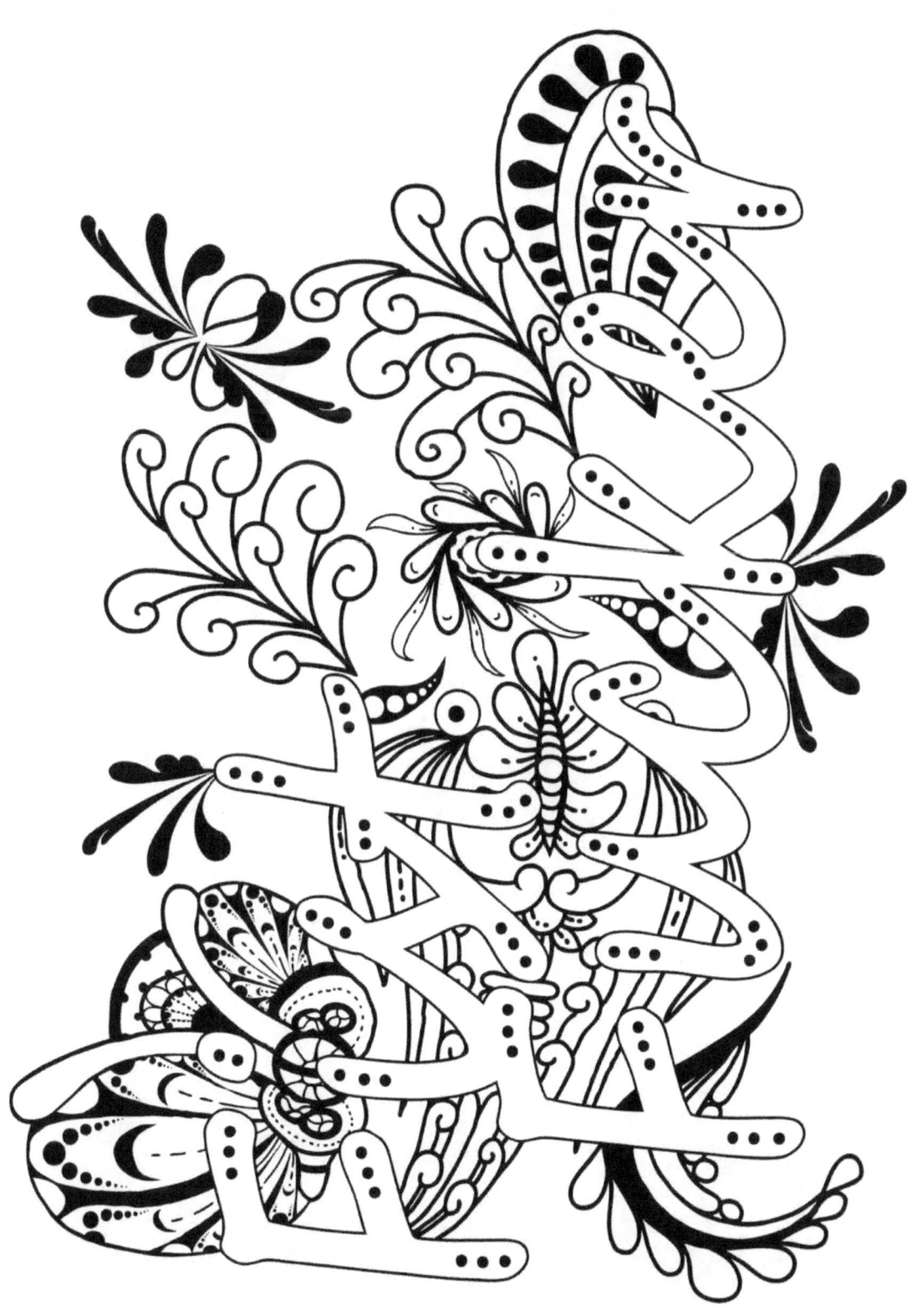

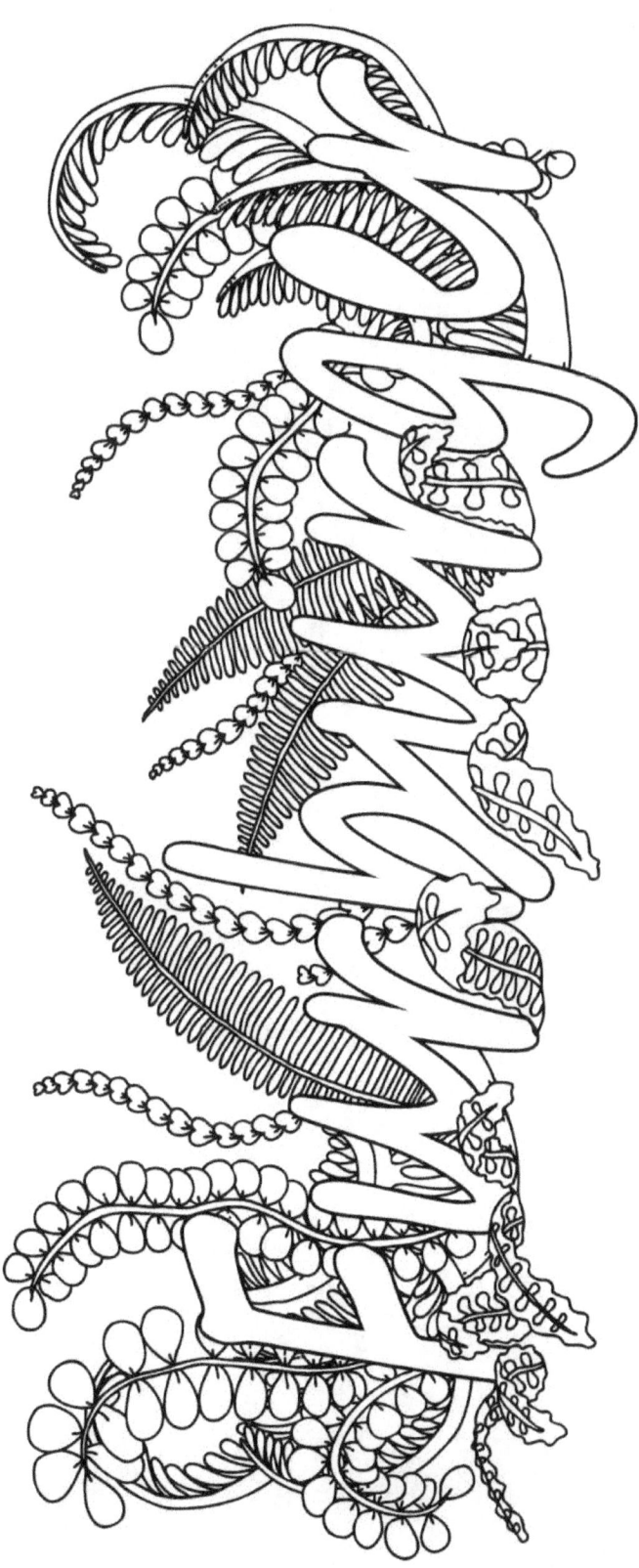

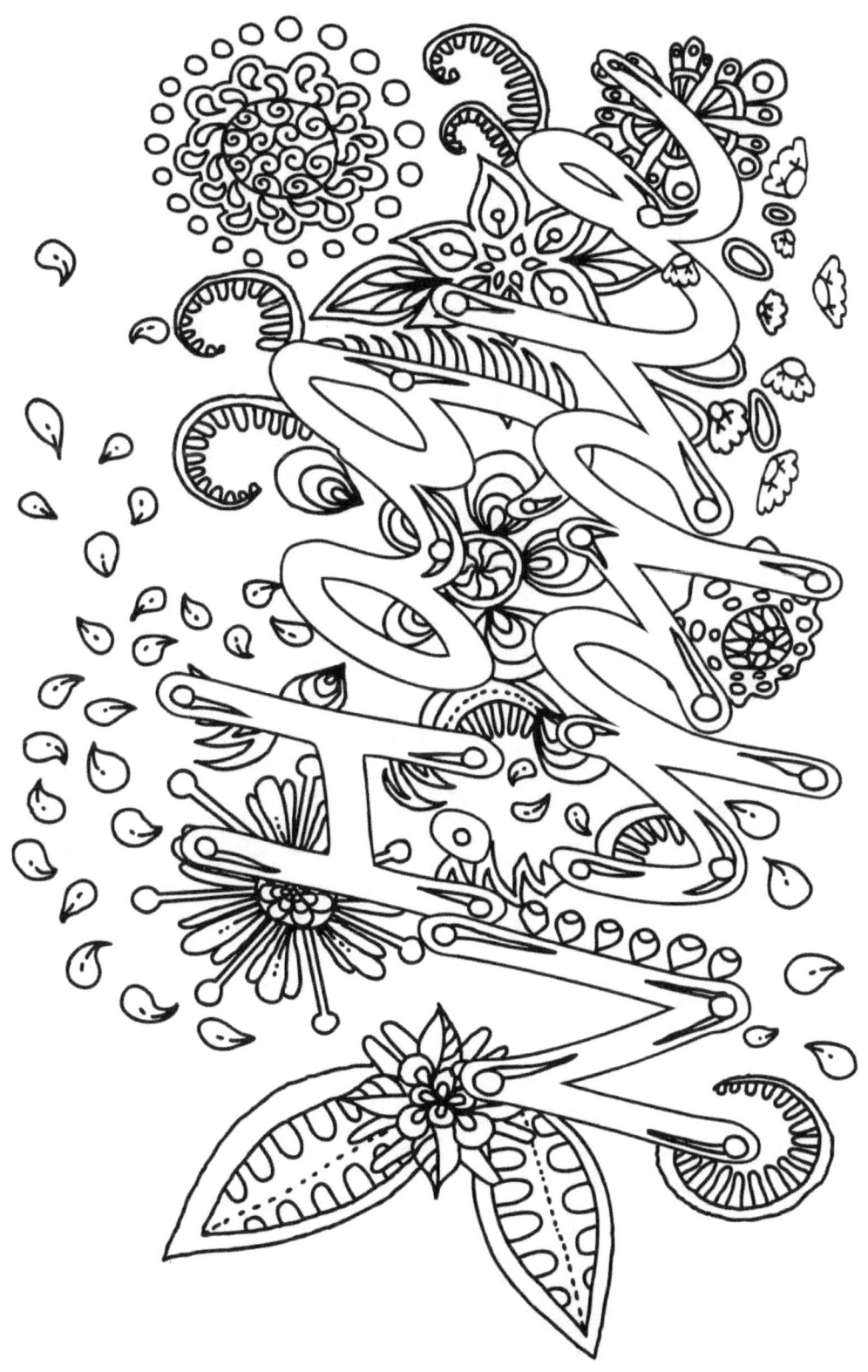

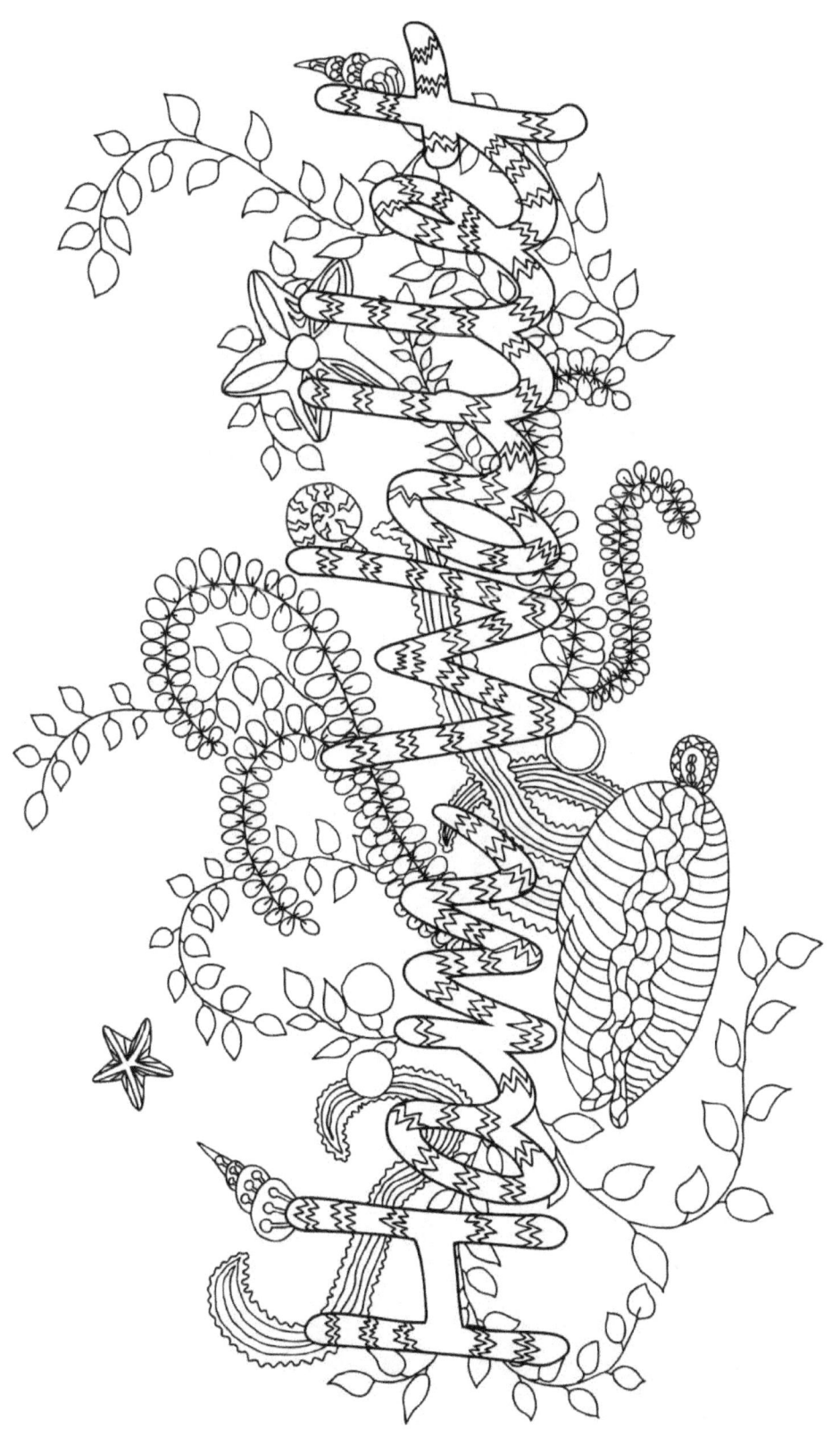

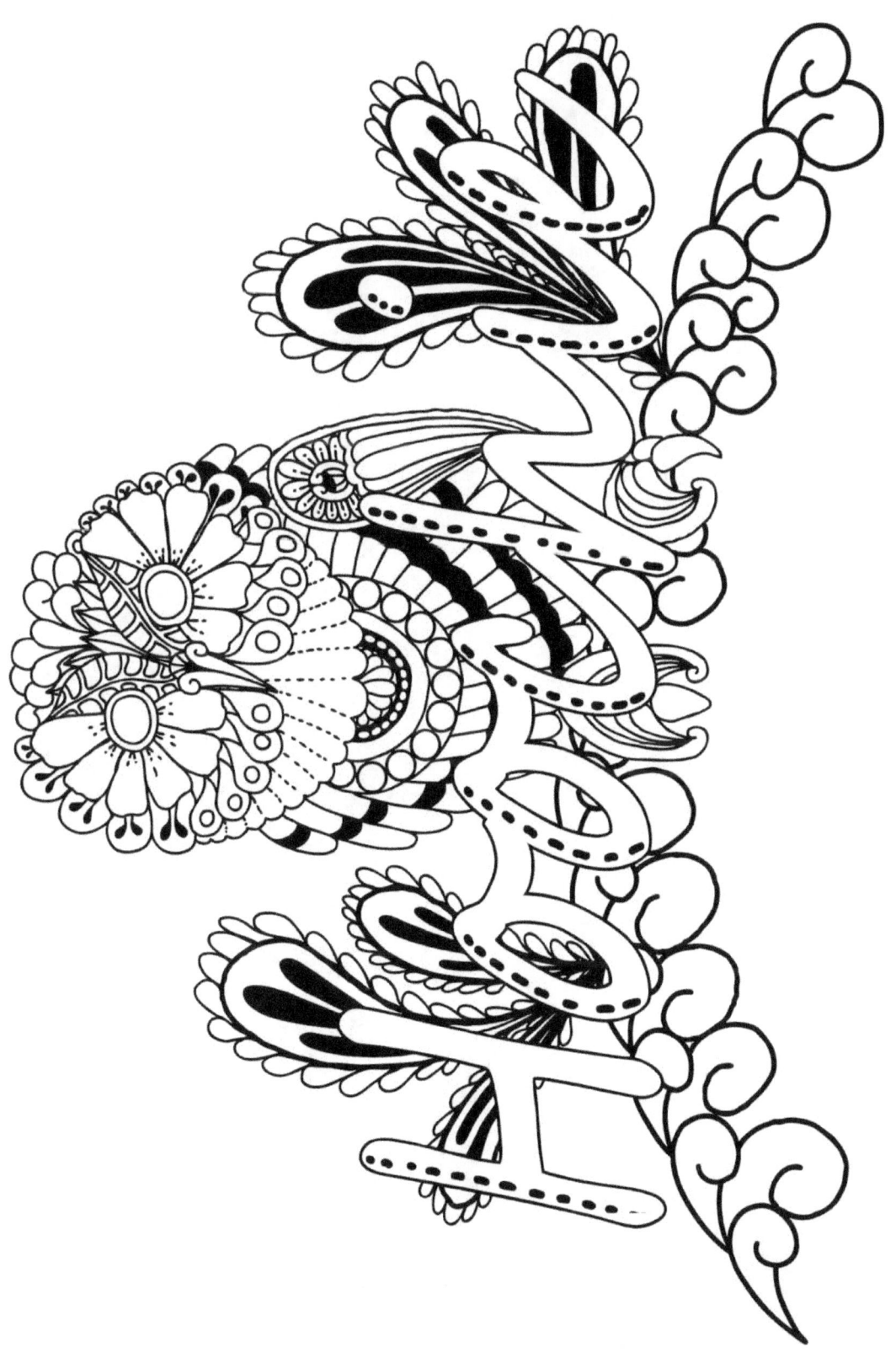

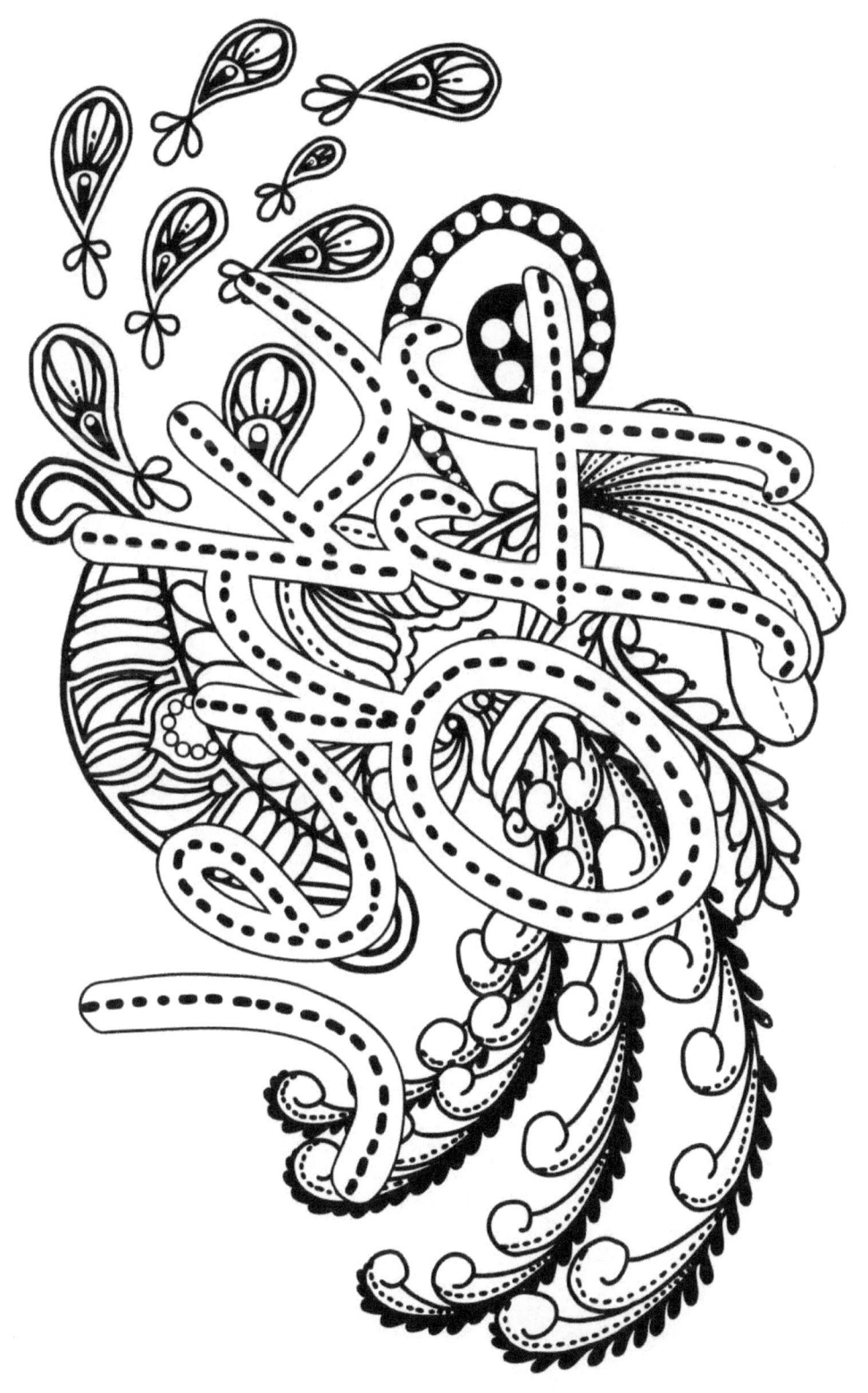

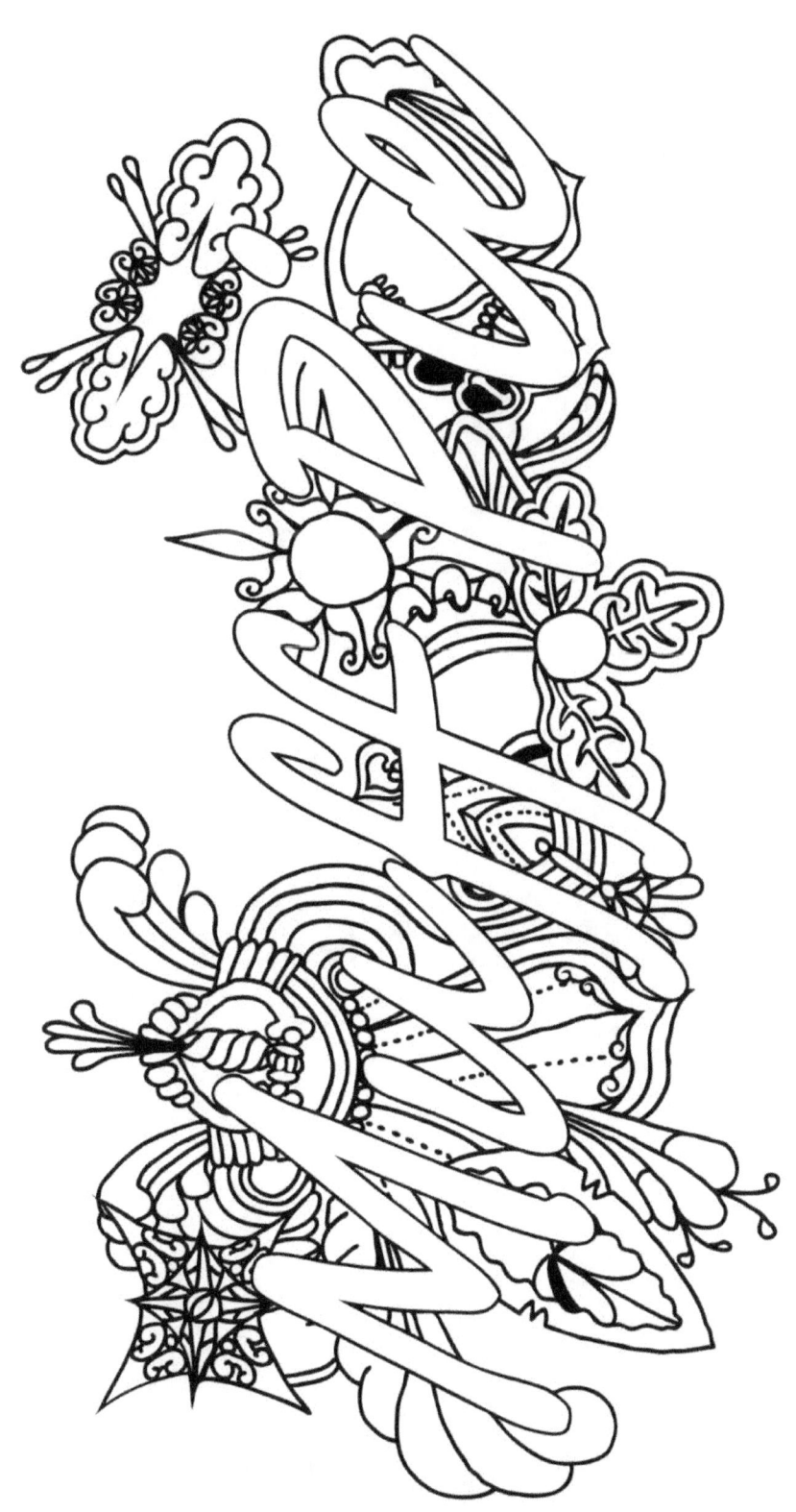

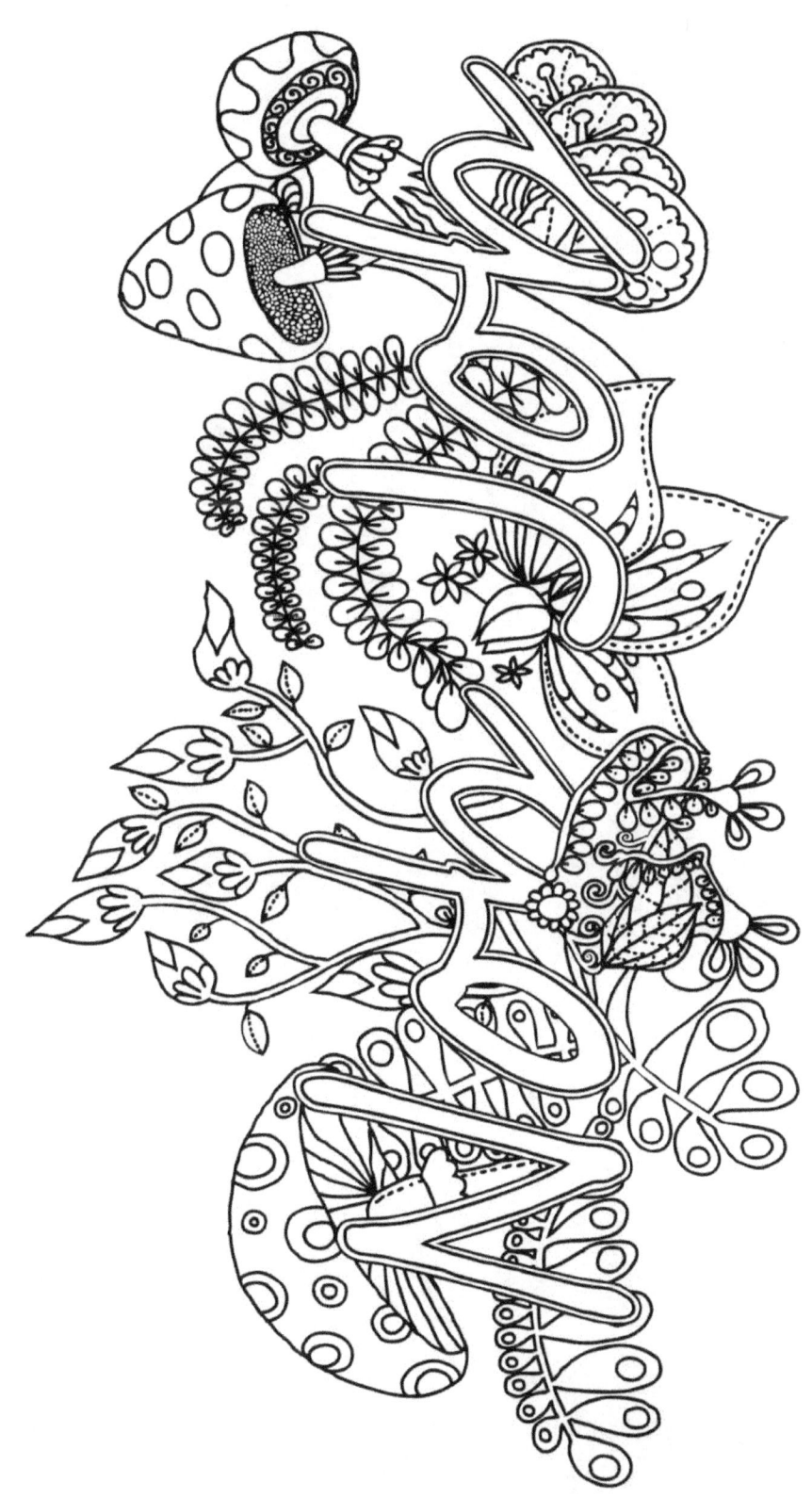

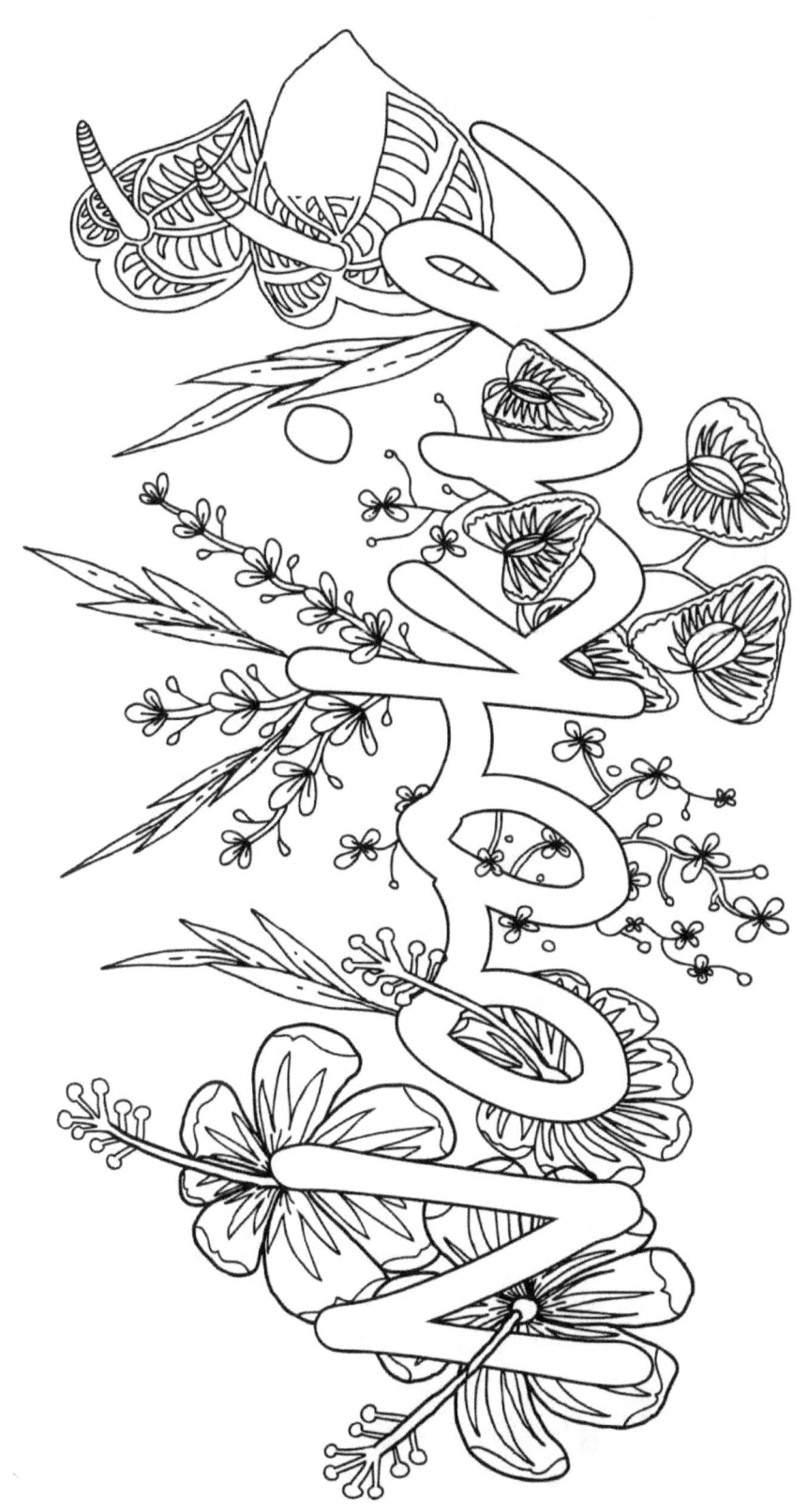

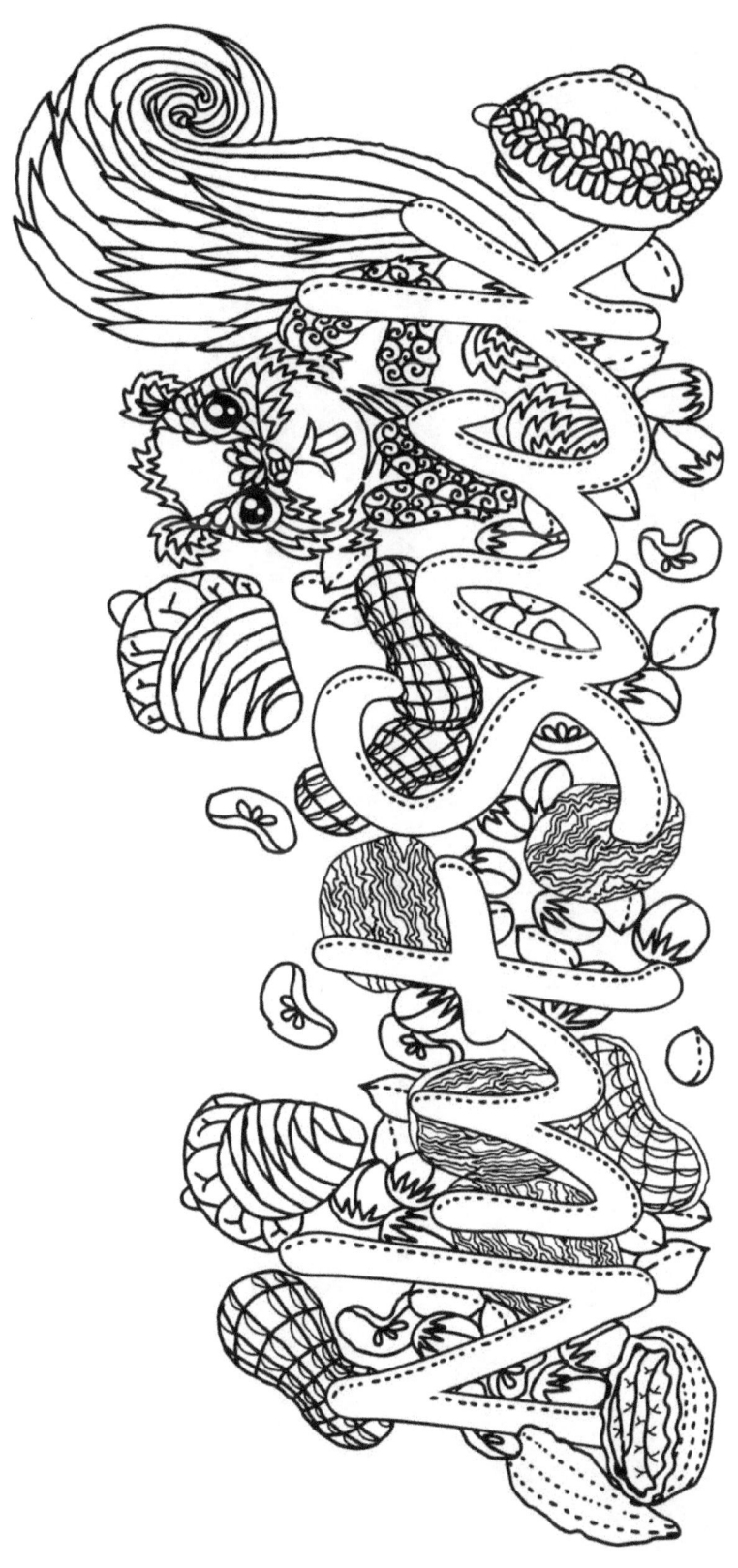

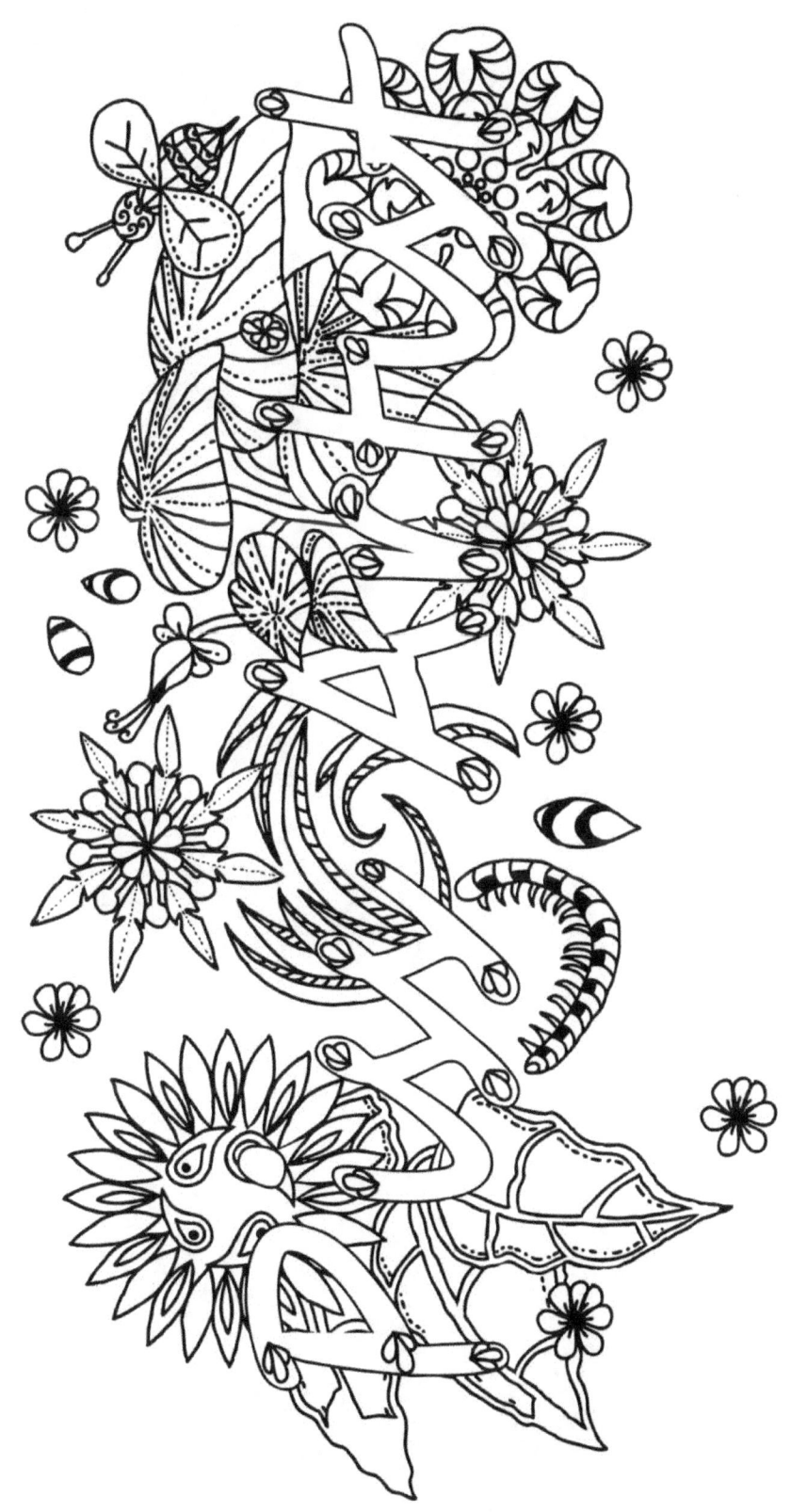

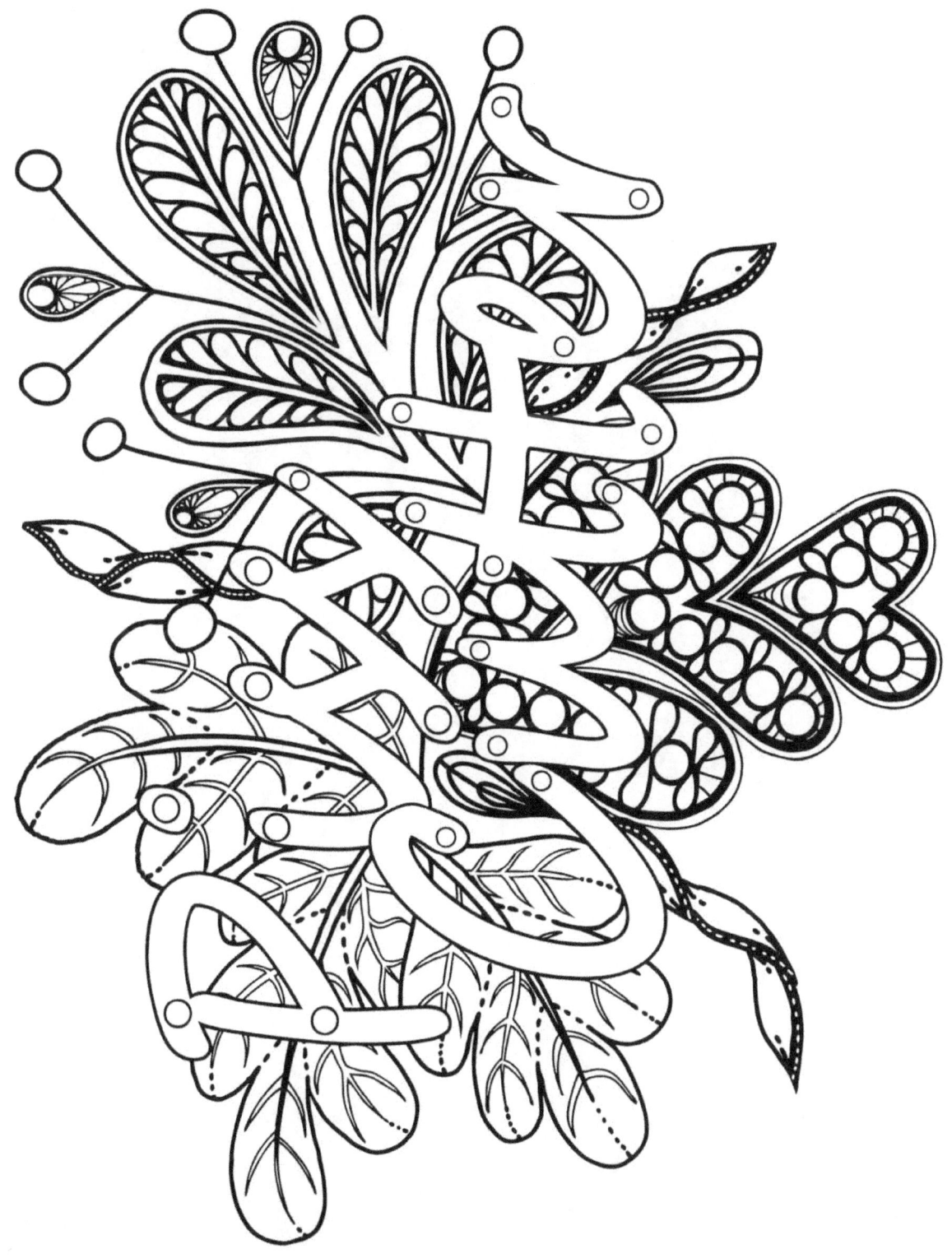

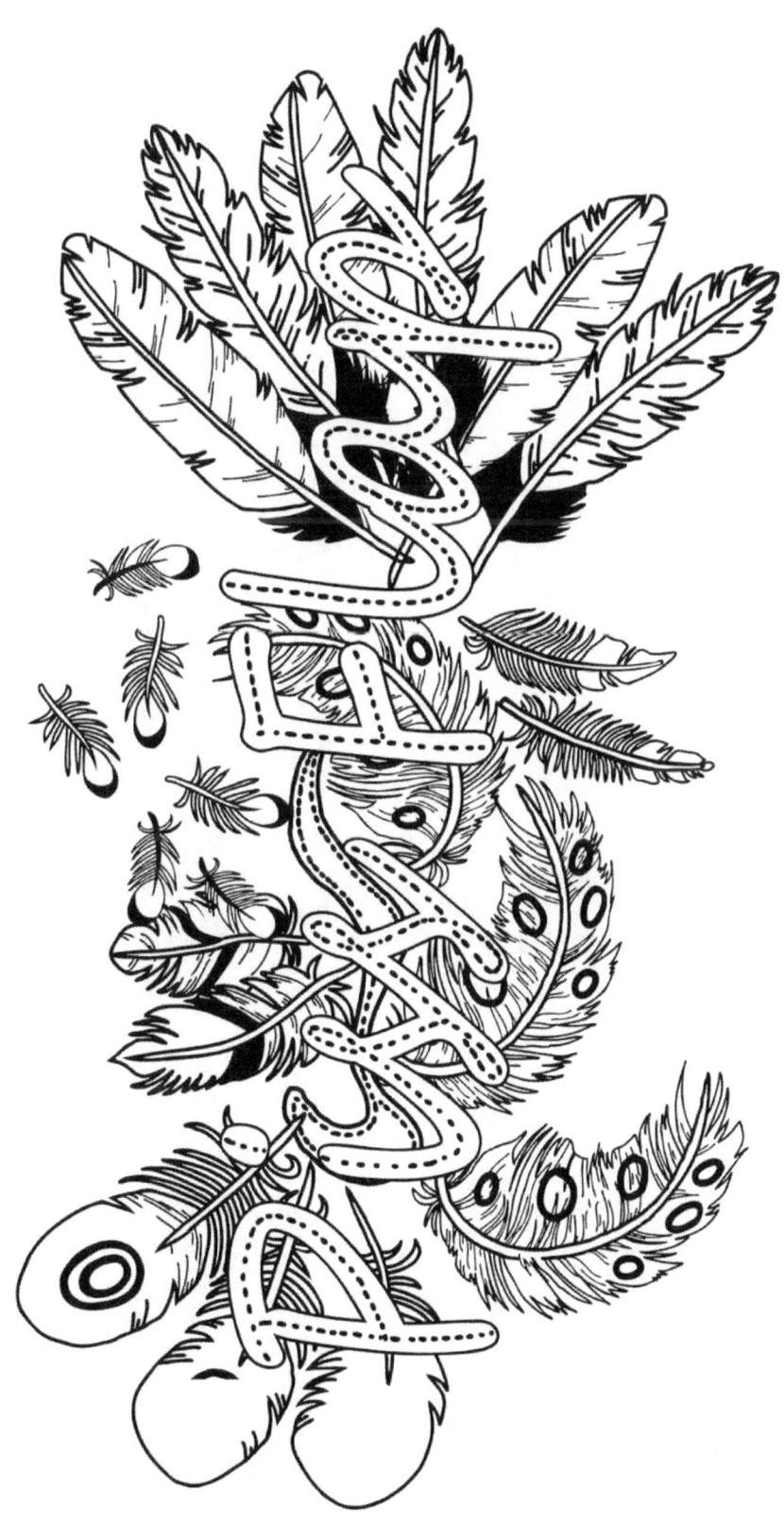

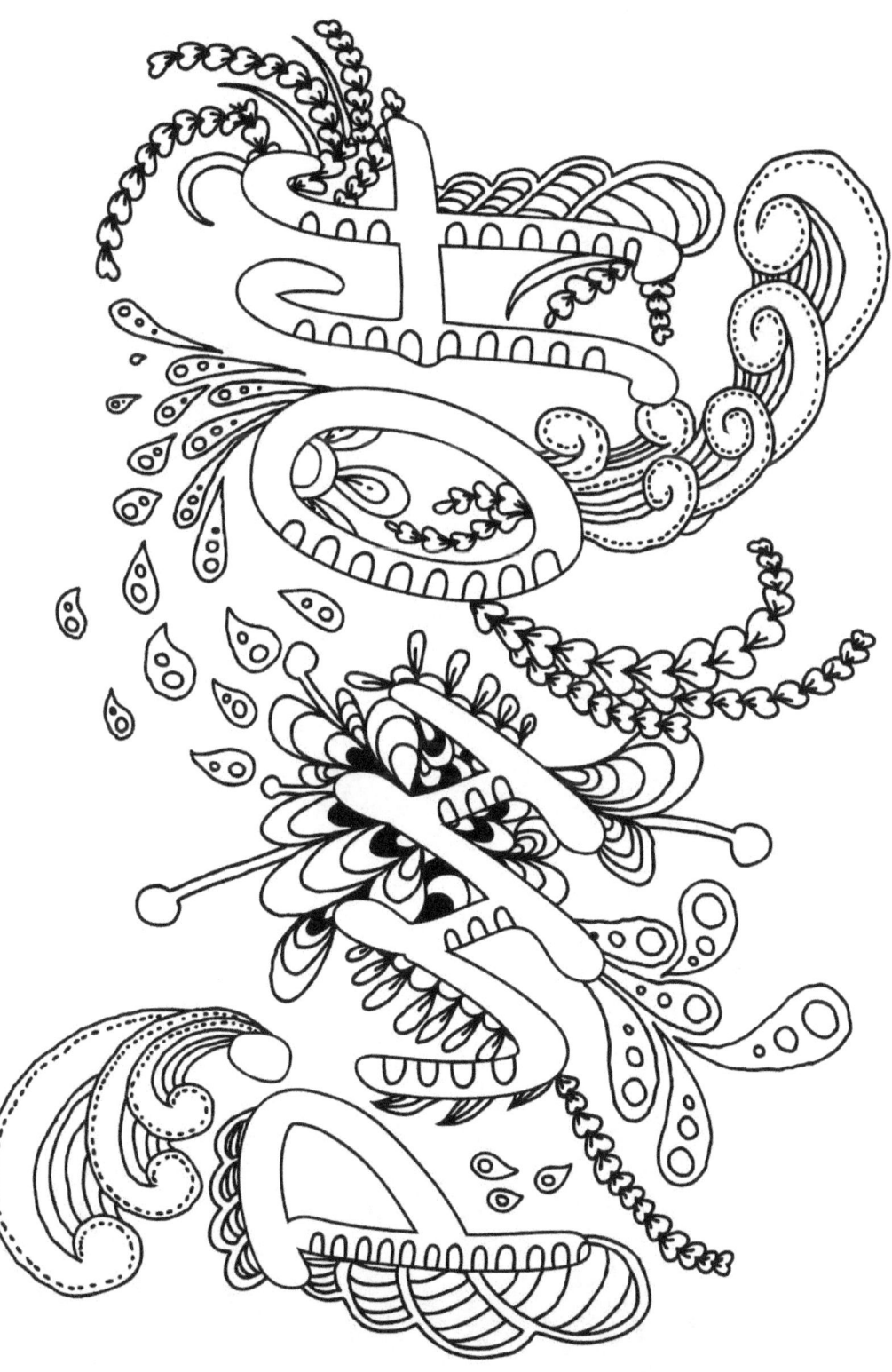

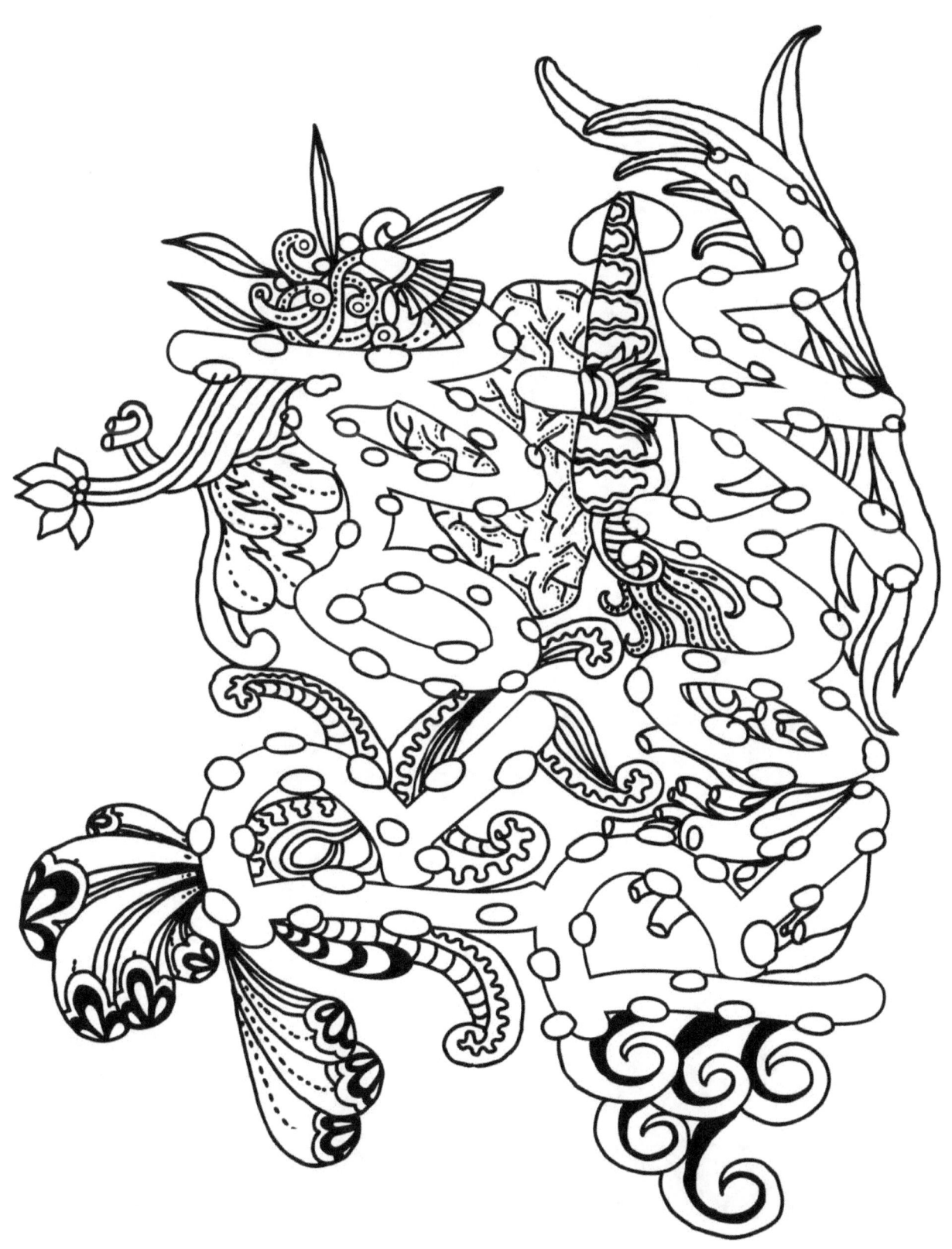

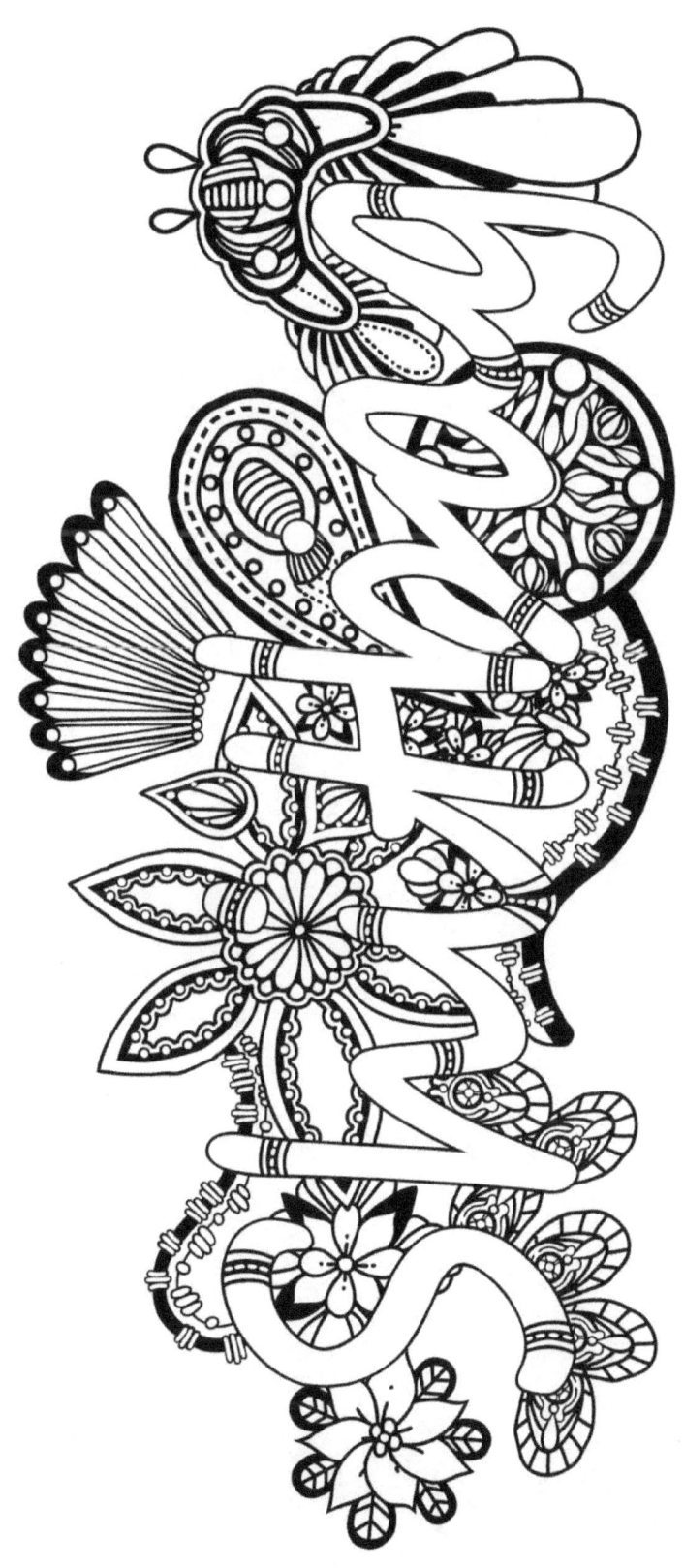

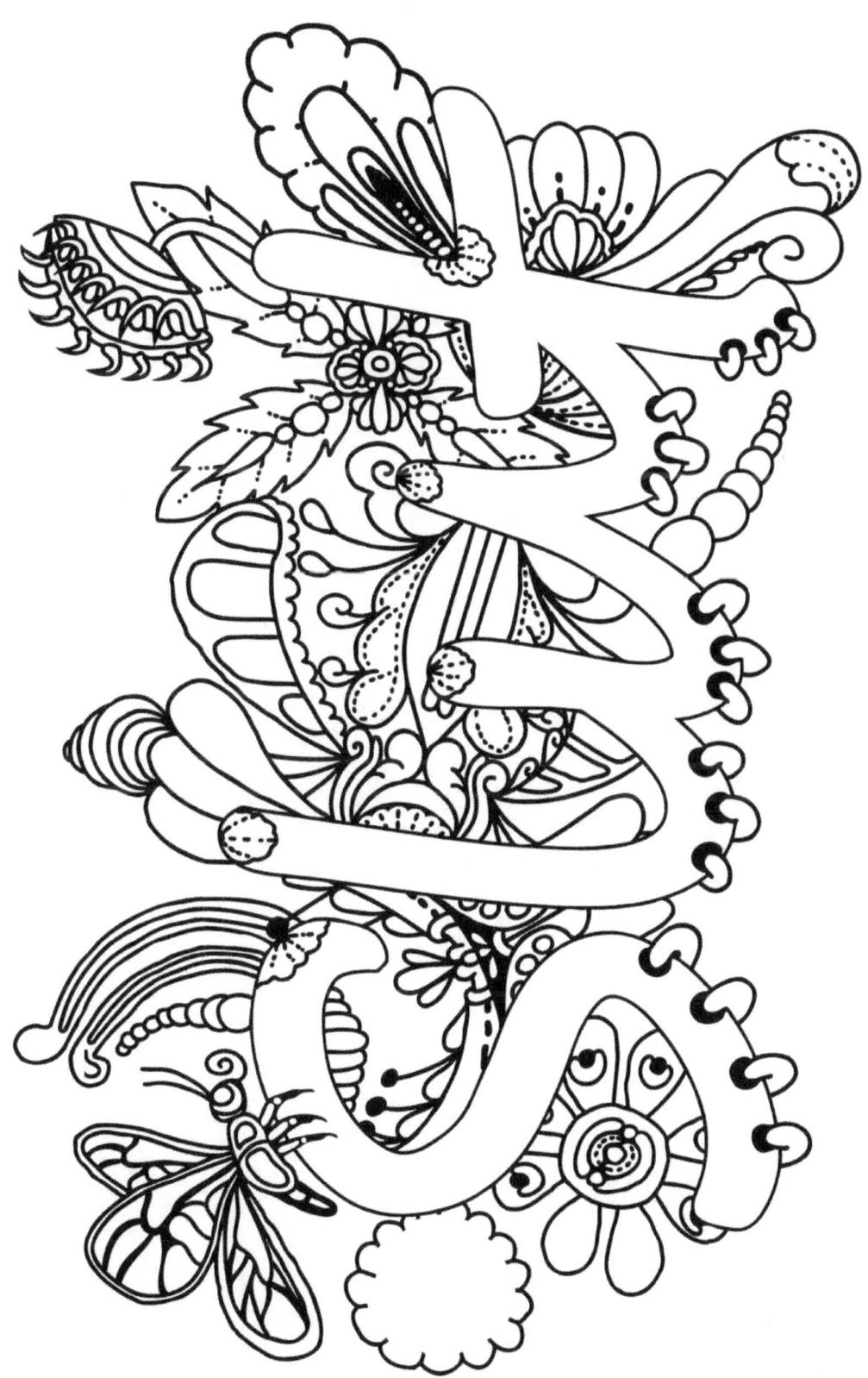

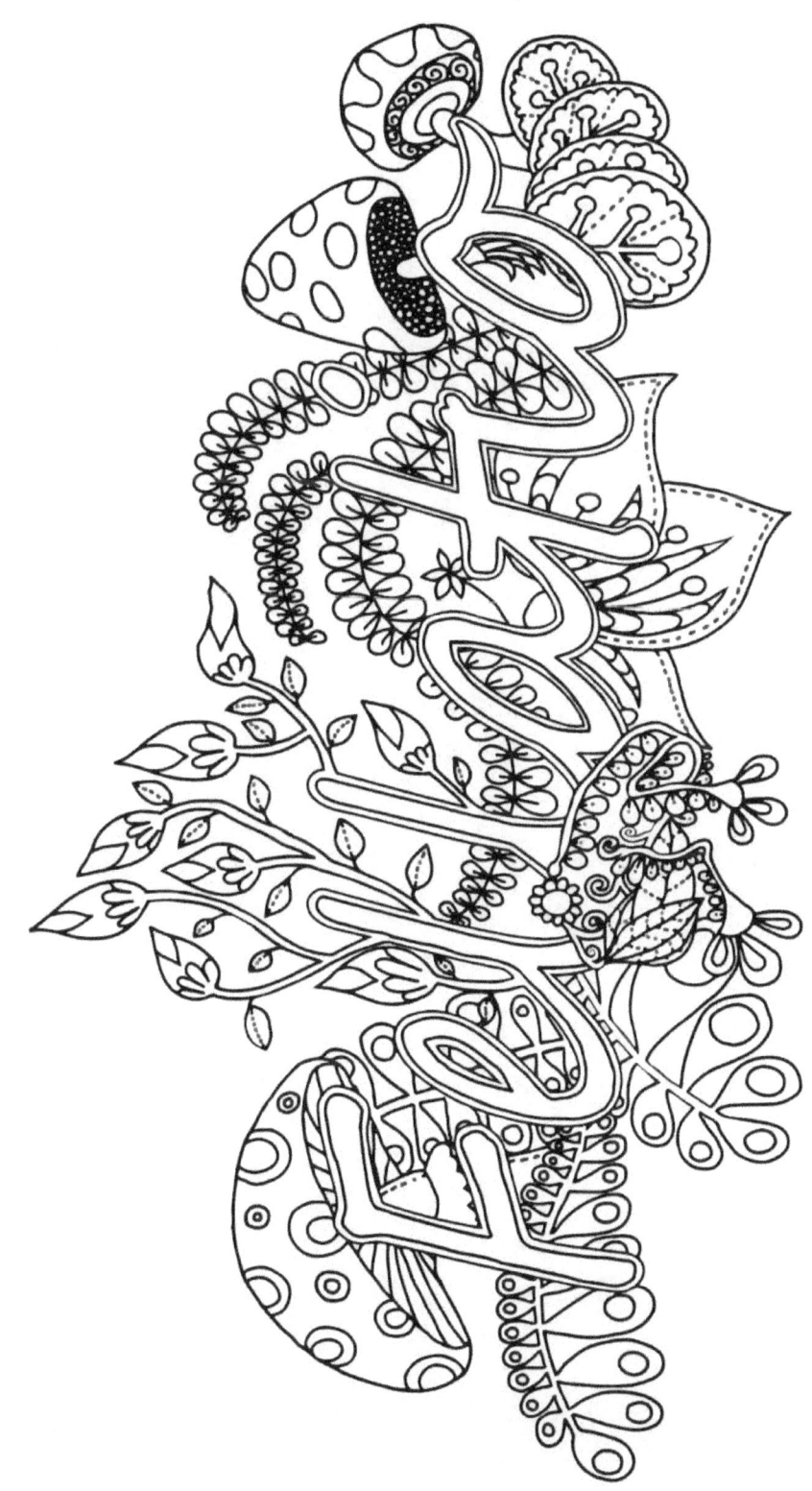

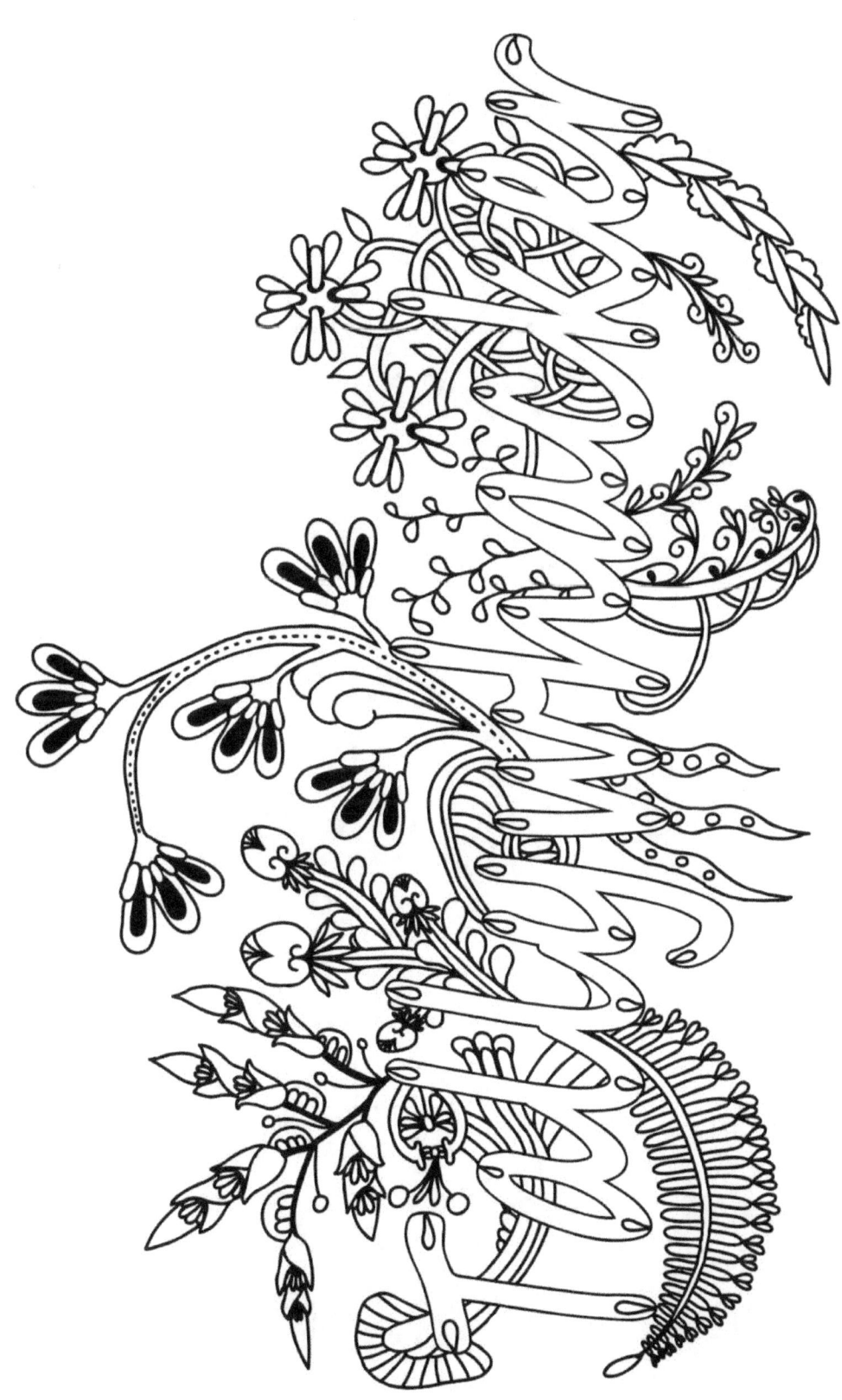

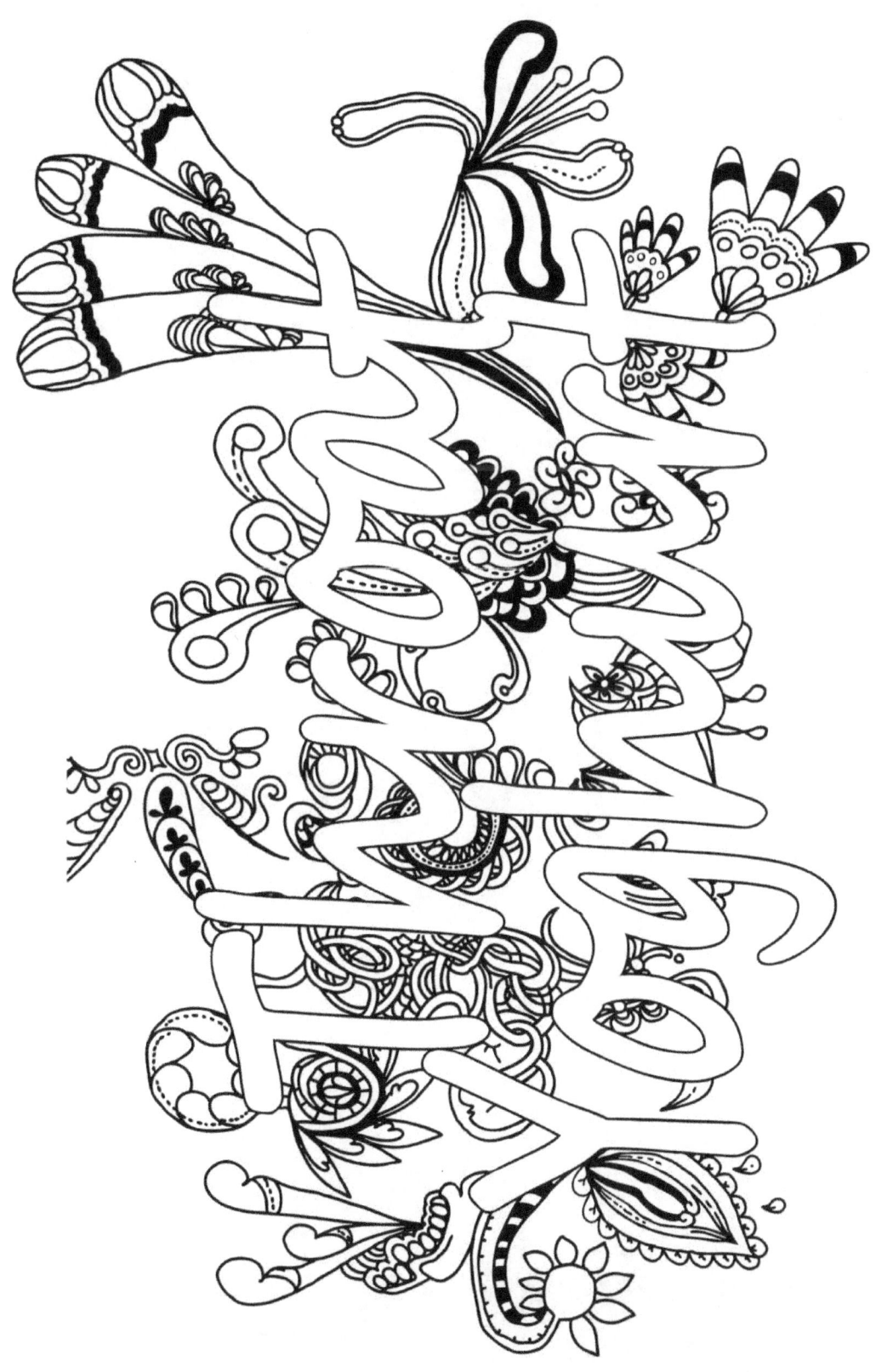

From the Author

Thank you for buying and coloring our book, we sincerely hope you have had fun coloring our naughty words ☺

Can we ask for a small favor? A lot of work goes in to preparing and publishing our books and honest reviews really do help us, especially when it comes to understanding what we should improve in our books.

If you have a minute, we would really appreciate if you could go to the book store where you have purchased this book and leave a short review…we do actually read our reviews!

Thank you!

www.ingramcontent.com/pod-product-compliance
Lightning Source LLC
Chambersburg PA
CBHW080628190526
45169CB00009B/3317